Love Whispers

Love Whispers

Swami Rama

The Himalayan Institute Press
Honesdale, Pennsylvania

The Himalayan Institute Press
RR 1, Box 405
Honesdale, PA 18431

8   7   6   5   4   3   2   1

Cover Design by Michele Wetherbee
Calligraphy by Nicky Ovitt
Photograph © Takashi Mizushima/Photonica

This book is printed on acid-free paper. ∞

ISBN 0-89389-178-9

To Her

Contents

Introduction

Love Whispers is the only work besides *Living with the Himalayan Masters* in which Swamiji does not hide his true identity. The joyous relationship between him and the Divine Mother finds its full expression in these pages because Swamiji had no intention of publishing a book when he penned these lines. For a long time its content remained hidden in the deepest chamber of his heart and between the covers of his personal diaries.

In the early eighties I was fortunate enough to read some of the letters Swamiji had written between 1956 and 1975 to Dr. S. N. Agnihotri, a beloved friend and disciple. And in those letters I saw in Swamiji a sage inebriated with the love divine, a sage who presented himself in the West as a scientist, a yogi, a researcher, a humanitarian, and an executive of a multi-national organization, the Himalayan International Institute. I was also lucky enough to be taking his dictation when he answered a letter from an astrologer in New Delhi. This astrologer, who was closely related to Swamiji's biological family, had written to warn Swamiji of a calamity which, due to the placement of planets and stars, soon would befall him. I still have a copy of Swamiji's answer. It said in essence that once the Divine Mother had given him Her unconditional love and protection and had placed him under the safety of Her lotus feet, why should he make any effort to protect himself from the movements of these planets and stars? As he was dictating this reply I saw in his eyes a light that did not seem to be of this world.

Such occasions were, however, very rare. Most of the time Swamiji seemed practical and down-to-earth. He seldom shared his mystical experiences with anyone. In every book he wrote and every class he taught he made sure that people heard his main message: "Be practical. Don't be emotional. Be nice to yourself. Take care of your duties. Live in the world and yet remain above it. Achieve the higher purpose of life here and now." I had been living in his company for several years before this book was published, and I was growing a bit tired of hearing him teach the same thing.

One Sunday morning Swamiji was scheduled to lecture as usual when, driven by *samskaras* or by Divine Will, I found myself in an unusually mischievous mood. Right before his lecture I walked into his quarters and found him putting his shawl around himself in preparation for walking down to the lecture hall. Without much thought I jokingly said, "Swamiji, I have just achieved a great *siddhi* [spiritual power]." When he asked what it was I answered, "Now I can read anyone's mind and I can predict the immediate future. I can tell exactly what you are going to say in your lecture."

Swamiji smiled and said, "OK, tell me."

I said, "You will walk to the stage in your regal style, go to the podium, and while looking at the audience, you will bow your head and say [and here I began to imitate his speaking style], 'I pray to the Divinity in you. How are you today? Are you comfortable? Do you like the food here at the Institute? If you have any problem, please tell Kevin or Dr. Clarke.' Then very gracefully you will walk to the blackboard and while looking at the audience you will say, 'A human being is not body alone, not mind alone. A human being is a breathing being too. . . . Here is body and here is mind.' Then you will draw two circles on the board and say, 'Between these two there is something called breath' while you connect the circles with arrows . . .'"

As I was about to complete the last sentence, Swamiji grinned and roared, "Badmash [rascal]! Are you making fun of your guru?"

I replied, "No, Swamiji. But all these years this is the only thing I'm hearing. Is this all that yoga and spirituality are about? Isn't there something more to it?"

"Then what is yoga?" he said, "You tell me."

I said, "What's the use of catching hold of the nose, breathing left and right and concentrating on the breath if just by thinking of the beautiful toes of the Divine Mother one can become absorbed in Her and find oneself in the consummate state that renders the joy of samadhi tasteless?"

With that I noticed Swamiji's eyes closing and his head swaying in a gentle circle. He sank down on a nearby chair. It seemed as if he entered a world that an ordinary mind cannot reach, and there he stayed for the next five minutes. When at last he opened his eyes he said gently, "Promise that from today you will not remind me of Her. For if you do so I will not be able to function, and my master has given me a task that I must accomplish before this body falls apart."

That experience touched me so deeply that I began to wonder who Swamiji really was. He would talk about the Divine Mother from time to time after that. He called Her the Lord of Life, but he never said enough to really convey the profundity of his relationship with Her.

Excited by my growing knowledge and understanding of Swamiji, I thought several times of writing about his mystical experiences, but I had to drop the idea when I remembered that he told me in 1976 that I could not write about him until 21 years had passed. Thanks to my dear friend Arpita, however, who had the skills to persuade him to let her edit some of his diaries and letters, today we have this slender volume, *Love Whispers*. It gives us a glimpse of Swamiji's personal vision of the love and beauty which, as his own experience showed him, are intrinsic to all that exists.

Before *Love Whispers* was published there was no way to comprehend the level of consciousness and the wisdom that this mystic sage of the Himalayas embodied. But now the experiences associated with exalted states of consciousness, which he always safeguarded in his diaries, are accessible to the fortunate readers of this book. After reading the text we can surmise for ourselves that Swamiji was simultaneously the citizen of two worlds: the mundane world of the senses, and the spiritual world of pure revelation. As he himself writes:

When the great merciful Lord gave me the vision of the whole cosmos, I began composing the inspirations of my life in deep contemplation. These have enabled me to comprehend the profound meaning of life. Now I understand the mystery of the creation of the universe, its sublime simplicity and perfect lyric. Thou hast revealed to me all the divine movements beyond the forms and names of this world. Thus I could sing the songs that always bring the inner awakening that translates my past convictions into living truths. . . . My beliefs are well-filtered by time. My ideas have crossed beyond the golden angles of the sun, moon, and stars. The bird of my imagination has flown beyond the boundaries of all galaxies.

After seeing what ordinarily remains unseen to human eyes, Swamiji rose above the confines of national boundaries, religious affiliations, and ethnocentric loyalties. Thus one day he noted in his diary:

I am a messenger, a child of the Himalayan sages. I belong to all nations and selfless service is the singular expression of my pure love. This is the fullness of life. It can only be reached by perfecting the relationship to the Self of all. . . . When it [civilization] embraces the Lord of Love as the very basis of living and being, what will be the fate of the priesthood? Who will go to pray in the temples and churches? There will be no multiplicity of shrines. Every human being's heart will become an altar of love. . . . Oh my fellow travelers, do not create a gulf anymore. . . . Wake up! You are still in the depths of sleep. You are captive in a solitary cage with no horizon beyond it. Come out of this imprisonment, for I am incomplete without you.

After *Love Whispers* had been compiled, edited, and was about to go to press, I remember Swamiji sitting quietly one night, seemingly immersed in the depths of a truth not yet known to us. The next morning he showed me a poem he had written the night before. Upon reading the first stanza I was elated, for it told me who he is and where he truly resided. But when I read the second stanza I felt as if I had been struck by lightning. It read:

> With snowy weather beating around me,
> Ascending the peaks of the mountains I go.
> No one talks with me, no one walks with me,
> As I cross streams and tramp glacial snow.

When I asked Swamiji what it meant, he replied, "I slipped into the future. This is the reality of the future. Don't feel bad—read the last stanza."

> Offering my life at thy holy feet,
> Loving all—selfless and complete.

As soon as I finished reading this final couplet, he said, "I love you and I love those who have surrendered themselves at Her holy feet. Safeguard the secret . . . by sealing your lips. Service is the way to be with me."

Swami left his body in 1996 but his love for the Divine and Her creation still whispers to our hearts.

Pandit Rajmani Tigunait
November 1999

Foreword

For many years, Swamiji has kept the habit of writing prose and poetry in his daily diary. Deep in the solitude and silence of dark night, when all the world slept, he would reflect on life or nature and note down his thoughts and insights—and he would record his dialogues with the Divine. He never allowed anyone to read his diary but kept it always with him. On rare occasions he would read an entry to his close students.

In 1984, when Swamiji was in Manali, in the Himalayas, to write *Perennial Psychology of the Bhagavad Gita*, he permitted his close disciple Swami Ajaya to see some of the entries in his diary. Swami Ajaya was deeply impressed with the beauty and profundity of Swamiji's writing, and was especially curious about Swamiji's love dialogues with his Beloved. He started asking Swamiji about Her, and Swamiji brought out his other journals, which contained more dialogues. Finally Swamiji revealed his experiences to Swami Ajaya by describing the visions he had been having of Her since the age of seven. Swamiji had not spoken of Her before because he wanted to preserve the quality of his experience by keeping it concealed within his heart, and he did not want his tender experience to be placed before those who might not understand or appreciate its sublime simplicity. Swami Ajaya assured him that the great poets and mystics of the past had also reported such phenomena and that seers have repeatedly described visions and conversations with their muse, ideal beloved, or blessed mother. He explained that Swamiji's rare experience would not be considered strange but would be acknowledged as transpersonal revelation.

Every era has been graced with a few blessed ones who see beyond the limited reality of the mundane and temporal. Those who dwell only on the gross surface of life cannot comprehend the profundity or subtlety of such a phenomenon. They tend to make light of it, subject it to crude analysis, or dismiss it as evidence of impossible fancy. Seers have therefore learned to remain silent about their visions, and Swamiji was no exception. But whenever he revealed a tiny glimmer of his experiences, his students were deeply inspired, and they gently encouraged him to share his private writings more openly so others could also benefit from them.

Being a literary secretary and disciple of Swamiji's, I persuaded him to hand over one or two diaries from among the many stacked in his personal library. Finally he agreed to offer his diaries for editing and publication; thus the work was assigned to me for compiling into book form. These entries are selections from 1979 to 1985; some were written in Japan, some in Nepal, and some in the Himalayas. Dr. Ballentine and Pennell Ballentine kindly gave us one of the letters that Swamiji had written to them, and we have included it here under the title "Love Offering." There are many more diaries, and Swamiji has consented to allow us to publish them also. This is the first volume of the series.

These poems, stories, and dialogues are exceptional in their beauty and spiritual depth. Reading them has an effect on the reader that cannot be described: they bring about a shift in perspective and expand the consciousness. This book is not to be merely read—it is to be reverently assimilated. Rarely do the unenlightened have opportunity to eavesdrop on the sage's communion with the Divine or to see life from his perspective. But in these prose poems, Swamiji has allowed us into the sacred intimate chamber where he dwells with his divine Beloved, and he has drawn open a curtain through which we may glimpse the interior world.

These prose poems reveal the devotional aspect of a great

yogic sage renowned for his keen intellect, practical scientific expertise, and selfless service. Known as a monist, Swamiji here describes reality from a dualistic perspective, conveying the true nature of mystical awareness and divine love. By sharing his inner reality, he has allowed us to glimpse that which is beyond the mundane and temporal. To him, this realm is as real as the phenomenal world is to us: he actually sees and talks with his visionary symbol of the Divine. Through these tender reports from the lofty heights of divine love, terse philosophical concepts are conveyed in a lucid manner. The heart simply opens to profound understanding beyond words. These sacred whispers of the night transport the loving soul to the realm divine.

Arpita, Ph.D.
Summer 1986

Love Whispers

It whispers from the heights,
It whispers from the depths,
It whispers from the mountains and the streams.
It whispers from above and from below,
   From the petals of flowers,
   From my little brooklet's flow.
It whispers from there and everywhere.
Love is a whisper divine.
But among all the whispers I have ever heard,
Her whisper is supreme,
   Fulfilling all my wishes
   And life's greatest dream.

§

Love Offering

From now onward, I will be a seeker of silence, and any treasure I find I will dispense with full confidence to those sincere aspirants who are treading the path. Long were the days of training I spent with my master, and I long to return to my deep-rooted habit of going into silence, ascending the mountains, and crossing the gliding glacial streams of the Himalayas. But if fate has to have it, let it. I will remain detached. I am a traveler, a witness, that walks on the path of light.

> Had light not fallen 'pon me,
> How little would I know!
> Dawn through darkness found me,
> And tickled by its glow,
> I rose and now must go.
>
> O sage that walks on light,
> O heaven that shines so bright,
> O dawn that brings delight—
> Farewell, my silent night!

Some people presume that I might cast off my physical garment, but that is not true. Now I want to gather all the scattered flowers of my feelings and thoughts and make them into a bouquet to present to the *deva** who is seated eternally on the altar of my heart.

I do not wish to dig a shallow well or sip the water of streams, but to drink the perennial nectar of immortality

*Bright being.

2

from the infinite ocean of bliss. In every breath of my life, I remember that sage who is the maker of exquisite melodies that vibrate from the chords of this little instrument. I am going to compose a song of soundless sounds in homage to that great one who has devoted his life in sharing the pure and beautiful—a man whose living faith has been a source of unfailing inspiration to me. In his memory alone will I offer the petals of the flower of my blossoming heart.

Now my hands and heart have started reaching out in his praise, and verily I have left nothing behind. His words have the abiding peace of a deep faith that accompanies a strange and joyful pain. There is indefinable heartache in the realization of this love, and a throbbing pain that finally ceases in blissful peace. This is an experience that cannot be narrated or communicated to others. It is an individual realization, and its fruits will be shared only with those who are prepared. My life is an open book, of which all the chapters are known to those who have been with me. It is a life of definite purpose and steady and ceaselessly selfless work.

Oftentimes when I ramble into the garden of my mind and into the fields of my consciousness, I gather the fairest flowers I can find and offer them to him alone who with his tender arms protects me. He is the architect of my life. As my thoughts dwell with admiration on his noble teachings, my heart leads me to the peak of ecstasy. I have a firm conviction that to realize the meaning of his teaching is to deepen the furrows from which shall one day spring a richer harvest of inspiration. Then I will be able to scatter the seeds of truth for the common good. I offer respectful *pranams** under the canopy of light poured upon me by the sky of the Himalayas. My soul flies to imprint a kiss of love and homage upon his venerable feet.

*Bowing one's head in a gesture of homage, love, and gratitude.

O Master, who in my tender youth
    Beneath a tree sat teaching,
Your voice upraised in prayer and praise,
Your words the means of solace bringing,
Now to thee my eager heart
    With love and praise is singing.

From now onward I will roam in the mountains to kiss the feet of hermits. My singing is like the enchantments of a bird's trill, and I will be understood only by those who are the students of nature and study its gospel. What does the bird do when rosy-fingered dawn puts life into it? Its awakening is not disturbed by the necessity of finding food. Its wings never fail to respond to the call of infinite space. Songs of joy it sings to the new morning light.

The day will soon come when my words will breathe not the musty fumes of the lamp but the fragrant aroma of the valleys of the Himalayas. My writings will not be confined to describing the imaginary exploits of the great heroes. I will follow the lead of the free thinkers and great sages on whom humanity counts.

I do not work for the applause of my fellowmen. I work because I must. The inner fire burns intensely within me and must find an escape. It does not matter if its warmth perishes unnoticed, light unseen. I have the conviction that true thoughts can be nurtured only in a free, friendly, and unfettered atmosphere.

I belong to no one but the boundless cosmos. Free thinkers and those who walk on the path of light are my brothers and sisters. This spiritual brotherhood creates a new bond that time cannot sever. It will instill into the young, impressionable youth the love for knowledge, and that knowledge will be absorbed, just as the young offspring receives with deep, silent devotion the tender loving care of its mother.

The music of solitude sings for me, and its echo resounds

4

through humanity and the universe. How wonderfully full of real life and intensity these sounds are in all their great variety. The music that fills the outer ear is but an echo of the inner harmony. One who learns to make his whole being an ear, alone hears the music of eternity. The unstruck sound, without drums and trumpeting, soothes my senses, stimulates my mind, and fills my heart. This inner music has consumed all the longings I had for external stimuli. How chaotic but exquisite!

Insight and imagination are my wondrous wands through whose powers I roam where I will. Silence is the source of all, from which the universal currents of thought flow spontaneously. I have been able to create a sixth sense—an inner ear. I am a traveler of three worlds, roaming without any bondage or care, though my permanent abode is the state beyond.

Fearlessness has now become my religion, for I believe that to lose something is to gain and to gain something is to lose. In actuality, there is no gain or loss: forms change, names change, but the existence remains unchanged. All transformations and transitions are trivial; there is no change in the absolute Reality.

I have been able to build certain convictions that have not been obtained from anyone but are filtered through my innermost visions. These gifts have been given to me by Providence, and they have been received freely by me. For years I cried in bewilderment in search of this treasure. When I looked at the heights and summits of the mountains, I found that they stand solitarily—all alone. By observing these heights, I realized that anyone who attains the heights remains alone. All great heights stand alone, but they are never lonely, for they are pervaded with the awareness that they are all in one.

I revere freedom immensely. My conception of freedom dawned, tearing the mist of loneliness that I occasionally experienced on the path. To me, the chains of sloth, cowardice, and ignorance constitute bondage no less than the yoke worn by an ox. I prize and insist upon internal restraints. Actually, freedom is based on inner happiness born of self-surrender, self-purification, self-control, and self-enlightenment. I have a burning desire to see each person's spirit free, to give it wings to soar high, so that it may have expansive vision and boundless space. Let everyone be ever open to new light. I continue to be a seeker of silence, searching for the deeper meaning of life to bring it forth so that it can be dispensed to console and comfort the weary suffering world. I believe that every moment of life should be useful, fruitful, and purposeful—in the world, through selfless service, and in solitude, through meditation and contemplation.

§

To Thy Glory

O little life stream, move on from this solitude.
I forsake all thy waters; flow freely and go thy way.
With all devotion thy flow be good;
My fellowmen will find thee after many days.

Once upon a time I sat on the mountain looking toward
the Ganges. The moonlit night paled its light on the silvery
sands, and a crying thought came to my mind from out of the
forgotten past, saying, "The joy that sits still with its tears on
the red lotus of pain grows in my heart." The gentle bird of
my spirit traveled far and beyond the golden angles of sun,
moon, and stars in search of Thee but returned back to its
abode unfulfilled. After a while I realized that the joy that
compelled me to dance on the dais of life's theater throws
everything it has upon the dust and knows not a word: silence,
silence, silence. The rhythmic dance of Providence compels
me to breathe—so I breathe. Since then in my life, joy and
sorrow are mingled into only one song, which I do not ever
sing. From that moment, I have experienced pain-mingled
gladness without measure. One day a ray of light suddenly lit
my being, and people who knew me wondered how my life
had been transformed.

O silent Divinity, Thou art a majestic queen among
women, a flame of light in the dark chamber of my being.
Why hast Thou forsaken me when I need Thee in manifestation? Nothing mundane—no beauty, no charms, no temptations—delights me. I tried once and twice to find fulfillment
in the temporal and failed. Thy revelation to me provides
great power and freshness to my mind and heart. Thou hast
given me glorious spirit to work day and night. That is how I
function.

I have never seen anyone who came so close to my ideal. Canst Thou deny that Thou art that? I worship not Thy form alone, but the light that shines behind the lamp. I respect with great reverence the architecture of Thy being, which is already ingrained in the bed of my memory. Thou art not subject to change, death, decay, and destruction.

I had the first vision of Thy glory when I was seven years of age. It shook my entire being. My whole body trembled, and I could not mutter a word in Thy praise. I was told that Thou art a golden light, a guiding principle, a guardian angel, a torchbearer on the path. That experience is as fresh and young today as it was in my childhood. Often I tried to paint the dignity that smiled on Thy face. Thy slightly olive-tinted complexion, luminous eyes, and long, wavy dark hair made me captive. Thy smile was gentle and spontaneously winning. The more I knew of Thee the more I saw that Thy face combined in a remarkable way humor-filled brilliance and unselfconscious dignity. How strange that death could not whisper her secret into Thy ears and could not change Thee. Indeed Thou art beyond all forms and names.

§

My Love

Art Thou an illusion, a vanity, a dream, or a phantom?
Art Thou a majestic mother that suckles me at Thy bosom?
Art Thou my Beloved, limited by no color, no attributes,
no form?
What happiness could be greater than Thee, my Beloved,
my Phantom?

So far, I have been terrified that it is only me who has been experiencing such overwhelming and overpowering beauty, and often I have felt that I was self-deluded and self-deceived. That is why I never even whispered this part of me to anyone. Today alone, with all my certainty, the clouds dispersed, and a ray of light gave me a new vision of courage. After all, what is reality? Is it a reflection of the human mind, of the collective mind, or of the transpersonal mind?

When I was seven years of age, I suddenly felt a thundering shock that transported me to a different realm of reality that I had not been aware of. Terrified, I approached my master, and he said, "There dawns something higher—something exquisite, implicitly wondrous, and unexplainable—so do not talk. Lay your hand on your mouth, and do not allow the secret to come out of the chamber of your heart, for anything that comes from the heart to the mouth becomes impure. Therefore, let it remain in the heart of hearts."

Since then I have been adoring Her on the altar of my heart and entering into dialogue with Her. These dialogues for me are always meaningful, and they answer all my questions and leave me free to write, act, and speak the way I choose.

Said She, "I must tell you that you must talk less so as to feel more, and you must not be carried away by the thought that everything could be forgotten and that you could easily sever the links with the past." To me, since then, recalling any event from the reservoir of the past is spontaneous. This recollection helps me a great deal and puts me on the path again and again.

Said She, "Do not be shy. Is it a calamity? It is actually nice. Why are you not sensitive? Perhaps instead of gathering, you have started scattering. Compose yourself. Do you know what exalted love means? If I really love you, in no way do I want to frighten or harm you, even if you think I have no form, no name, no attributes."

I am afraid that this kind of vision envelops me with a limitless love that agitates my mind and turns terribly quickly from civility into impudence. "I am a man. I would flee to the ends of the earth simply out of reverence for Thee, rather than to remain discordant with Thee, for Thy love always gives me new perspective and shows me light. This is not mere talk."

Said She, "I assure you that I know you and love you exactly the way I know and love Myself. If you fail to find your happiness now, it will be difficult for you to find it later. If you do not find yourself completely happy and resolved, you shall ruin everything—your talents, your feelings, and all that you have. I love what is honest and good. Try to calmly put yourself in My place and think—do I not rejoice to look upon you? Love is a great amulet, and you are assured by Me that you will always have it. So guard it zealously, never speak of it, and do not go to extremes." Bidding 'bye, She said, "I love you."

§

My Phantom Lady

Love ties for mortal beings are always molested by the wild ambitions and biological necessities probing into the depths, with psychological curiosity mingled with recognition and some gratification. Love for the Divine is higher than love for human beings. Love for objects is inferior; love without an object is true love. How wonderful, how amazing, it is to realize that the divine essence of the Infinite enjoys being in this finite vessel. I believe that love, the living principle of the universe, is the all-pervading influence that redeems the human from the desolate world of despair.

Having realized this, the joy of my faith has inspired me to pour all my heart into the colors of Thy loving nature. I have found that in the heart of disappointment there is always seated a limitless joy that can emancipate one from sorrow. The acknowledgment of love as the guiding force of the universe is slowly moving in my inner being to disintegrate the gigantic mountain of my individuality, which is crumbling and slipping into the valley of limitlessness. True it is that when a sudden change in inner life occurs, the life force seems to suffer, and momentary pain appears. Yet I have hope against hope that the life force, after traveling upwards, attains perfection.

It is with this faith I live. It is this irresistible force that remains busy in shaping the course of the world. The burden of this awareness weighs upon me, and I cannot carry it alone. May I share it with my fellowmen?

I heard a voice saying, "To get fire from wood, you have to burn it. To create a sacred flame, you must intensify your endeavor." There is always fire within you. You can gather or scatter. There is a constant battle going on in the human heart and mind to light this fire. When I am inert, I am parched and bare, but I feel no pity for myself. Breaking is a fierce kind of getting, and parting is a kind of meeting. But this is only poetic imagination. I am haunted by my sense of weakness. I know Thou art not a mirage. Please do not part from me, for this tiny vessel will cry.

O Divinity! Without Thee this life will enter into essential hollowness. Whenever I tried to approach Thee I heard an emphatic "No!" As a result of my full determination, will, and perseverance, Thou wilt one day unlock the door to the city of life. My secret of life is to tread the path of surrender and not conquest, and not at all renunciation. What a joyful pain I experience. How long in this tragic manner will this little brooklet flow through these dense woods?

Life seems to be brief and the task vast. This tragedy has become a part of everyone's life. There is a constant struggle between actual life and the dead rules of the world in which we live. These dead rules are the source of our movements in the world today. This conflict has obscured the light of love. Some call this flame the fundamental motive force of the universe, and some call it the creative aspect and guiding thread of human evolution. I have the courage to firmly hold this flame in the depths of my heart. Never I believed in man-made laws, neither in those artificial standards that ignorant society sets up. From these spring the human tragedy. Human endeavor is dashed, and human beings have become the slaves of man-made injunctions.

I have been waiting like a tired mountain to have a glimpse of Thee. Yet the pull of the mundane brings me back to the world of objects. My love, which can reach the lofty heights of the eternal, sometimes stoops down to dry a tear that is like a transparent glittering drop suspended on the eyelash of the child still full of sorrow but already smiling.

Thus spoke the Lady of my dreams: "How shall your eyes take meaning or measure of truth? Will faith ever feed, virtue comfort or keep you warm? What bewilders you, my love, that you wait for these phantoms to soothe you who are greater than spirit, you who are action and form? Then go your way, seeker, to your doom if you cannot be guided. Ride on the top of the world self-deceived, self-deluded, and cry your impossible cry. Must you choose your own way? In all circumstances my blessings will help you. May your life be as perpetual as the movements of the moon and the sun, equivalent to the longevity of the Himalayan Mountains. I come from the land where there is no unrest, where no jealousy stirs, where none are harassed. A heavenly peace envelops and encompasses all. Be still so that you feel more. I can lead you to the summit of ecstasy."

I gazed upon Her self-illumined face and said, "I wander along the banks of song and gliding streams. Under summer stars I listen to the gentle words of Thy wisdom. Thus my life has been shaped anew into a poem, poetry, and song. I thought life had reached its goal and final harmony had been attained. The old dream of paradise had become a reality. Nothing could be more congenial to me than my attitude against the rigidity of classical rules. I am always the breaker of bonds and of fettering traditions, but never the destroyer of their true basis. The great ones always created their rules according to the times, and I tread the same path."

Gazing upon her I wondered, How does this beautiful angel flit in and out of this world of form? Can I capture Her with my love? She whispers the tidings of the boundless unknown beyond. She is my Love of love, exquisite beauty, my phantom lady. My heart would feign hold Her near to itself but cannot, for She is formless.

This realization, the result of intuitive contemplation, continued, and I again entered into a dialogue: "Mystic being from the subtle world, had I not received Thy love, I do not know what shape the rest of my life would have taken. Thou revealest to me the melody and the magic of the deeper realms, with all Thy loving care. Thy soul comes and goes as a messenger in this world from the shore of the ocean of mystery. It is Thee of whom I now and then catch a glimpse in the dewy autumn morning, in the scented night of spring, in the innermost recesses of my being. Sometimes I strain skyward to hear Thy eternal whispers."

A burning desire lives in my heart, an earnest longing to realize the Infinite in the finite. An unceasing endeavor to explore the limits of the limitless is a dominant theme of my life. Mere forms and names of the world are amusing but not fulfilling. *Satyam, shivam, sundaram*—peace, happiness, and bliss—is the only goal of my life.

§

Golden Footprints

"Listen to me," said She, "Extraordinary skill and talent is rarely found—only in the gifted fortunate few. They have the capacity to pull the subtle strand from the Unknown and connect with the known. Thus they have the vision to explain both the known and unknown parts of the manuscript of life. From known to unknown is the accepted language of science, but here hails the profound language through which the Unknown is explained and brought to the known. Poets and seers touch the Infinite and connect the missing links of life by composing their inspirations and singing the songs of the Eternal. There is only one unbroken thread, which is endless, and that is called life. This endless thread leads one to the fountainhead of the Infinite, to its unmanifested state where we finally meet. There is nothing good or bad; there is nothing complete or incomplete. We are all marching to the essential unity, which seems to be obscured by the idea of diversity. Beneath all diversities lies only one unity, in which the lover and beloved both lose their individuality, and only love exists.

"Stop crying, for the pangs of separation are no doubt painful but momentary, too. When you have discovered your fate and destiny, the ultimate Reality, all your sorrows and pains will turn into joy and happiness. The path of love here is separation, but on the summit it is inseparable union. Go on treading the path without any fear of failure. One day you will reach there.

"Are you afraid that you will be consumed by the wild exaggerations and motivations that are dormant in the bed of the unconscious? Are you afraid of the temptations of the mundane and temporal? This fear is valid, but if you are a lost lover of the Lord, nothing can obstruct your way. Love, love,

love is the only self-existent reality. Is it with object or without object? The highest of all loves is love without an object, and if you have attained that height, you will not slip into the valley of dissipation. On the path of love, temptations do create distractions, but you also receive the blessingful blossoms left by those who have already trodden the path. Realize this and follow the golden footprints of those who have gone ahead."

§

Resolution

I am an ancient traveler of this universe. On this path of mine I find astonishingly interesting subjects to study, and I am the most conveniently available and comprehensive of all subjects. Those who are linked with me emotionally also become an inseparable part of my study. It is the study of self in all dimensions. This is a reality I was able to comprehend for my own contentment.

I said to Her, "My method of knowing is not that of Thine, for we live in entirely different realities. Yet I want to communicate. Let us understand both realities as they are and not shy away for fear of loss of one's reality. Love is the only link between the two realities."

Said She, "Though you are curious to know Me, I am not curious to know you, for I already know you well from My own perspective. Will you listen to My words uttered through My own lips, or do you want to draw your own conclusions about Me from the sayings of others and the opinions expressed by those who do not know Me at all, but speculate and project their own views and then say, 'Thou art this.' Life is like an untold story. It is without beginning or end. Death and birth are two avenues, and I am the ancient traveler going through these avenues again and again. Life is like a manuscript whose beginning and end are missing. Most people only know the middle portion of the manuscript. In the far past, cruel nature in her chasm split my soul from the whole and made me an individual. Now I am making efforts to become one with the whole. As you stand before Me, a mute exchange of thought takes place between us. You dismiss it, and I accept it with all My spontaneity."

I was profoundly stunned to hear Her voice. I had to create

a space for wanting to fill the space that divides us into two. It was necessary for me to do that. The painful demarcation had been immensely useful. For many days I could not eat, because any food immediately repelled me.

When I arrived at my Himalayan cave the view looking out from the cave was so vast that my eyes could not grasp its immensity. Disappointed, I began wondering, for it appeared to me as if my joy and the whole world were a small prison.

I said, "Many a time, with sovereign gesture, Thou didst pour the contents of Thy chalice into my mouth. Thou didst tempt me and disappear all of a sudden. I adore the words of Jesus, 'Lead us not into temptation'—but I say, 'Quench my thirst so that I remain fulfilled and therefore am never tempted again!' From this experience arose the thought that awakens me, and I dream dreams of Thee whenever I go to sleep. I am still thirsty. O my Love of love, do not be a symbol of inflexibility. Be gentle and generous, for this lonely traveler will be lost and there will be none to soothe."

I have climbed the summits of my life and measured the depths of the ocean of my heart. I have experienced that polarity which is composed of two differentiated ideas that we are. Indeed they are different, but they grow from one and the same soil. From this source also arises the dilemma that I alone have to resolve.

I said to Her, "I trust Thee with all my being, but I am longing for Thy union. I want Thee to manifest as a mortal being, but Thou canst not—or I want to ascend to the realm where Thou dwellest, but I cannot. Tell me, why art Thou silent? There gleams a ray of hope that one day merciful Providence will hasten to my aid, and Thou wilt be unable to resist."

I am torn and tired. Sleep wants to take me to her blessed bosom. I feel restless. When I begin to think in a clumsy way and decide that everything proceeds out of my intention and out of myself, then my childlike innocent heart assumes that it knows and knows that it knows. Yet all the while I am fatally handicapped by the weakness of my conscious life, for the corresponding fear of the unconscious has baffled me many a time.

Have I to begin again? This burning desire is not capricious. It lives with me as a constant substratum of my existence. It is as real as the physical world around me. It assails me from without and within, with overwhelming force from which I receive inspiration and revelation.

I am still thirsty. This thirst leads me from one land to another. I crossed many a mountain and river, visited and passed through the crowded abodes of mortal beings, but nothing was comforting, for momentary comfort is a temptation and not fulfillment. This thirst leads me to that sort of dissatisfaction in which I am always content but still unsatisfied. I walk alone, all alone in search of Thee, holding Thy love secretly. I am lonely for Thee.

§

Separation Is Brutal

The transition from this mortal earth is indeed a frightful and brutal experience. Illusions and delusions seek to hide and cover over the intense pain of separation, but for most the terror remains deep within. When a human being travels through the valleys of the known and unknown, real and unreal within himself, he finds that his attachment to the people and objects of the world is temporal and the mother of all delusions. The mortal ones do not realize this, but sages do. We all know this, but we do not realize it consciously. When someone separates from their loved one, in reality there should not be pain because separation is more real than meeting. The human soul has to travel all alone until he meets the Absolute. But selfishness and attachment contract our consciousness. When consciousness expands, pain vanishes. Eternal joy appears. The ascending power in the human being can meet the descending power which is normally beyond the human grasp. Others call it grace, but I call it a joyful wedding. This exquisite festival of life was never consciously celebrated before.

My endeavor is preparation for transition and an expansion of that sorrow from which springs the joy that prompts me to say what I want. Separation is deadlier than death. It is an actual experience of death while living, but then separation confirms my idea that the parting moments are moments of gathering, and separation a step forward to meeting.

Whispered She, "Separation in disguise is union, exactly as death in disguise is life. You should learn to love separation and death the way you have learned to love life. The one who makes truce with death in this lifetime crosses the mire of delusion, and the journey becomes painless."

§

The Vessel of Life

Today is a gloomy day because of torrential rain trying to sweep away the golden moments of my dreams. So often, jealous Nature comes between Thee and me and creates a barrier for a while. When I open my eyes, still overwhelmed with my dream, suddenly I become aware of the remaining years of life. It is unusual for me to think this way.

The vessel of life is well sealed with the years of expectation. This vessel has been the only burden that I carry with me. I vividly heard a voice coming from the depths of the vessel: "Accept me, my love, accept me." Curiously stunned, exceedingly astonished, I became aware of the drops of the wine of life crying plaintively from the depths of the vessel. But I was helpless, for had I unsealed the mouth of the vessel, its drops of nectar would have evaporated into empty space. The suspense, a conflict mingled with curiosity, prompted me to realize my helpless state. Neither was I able to resist the temptation nor was I able to unseal the vessel, yet I was unbelievably anxious to drink the rest of the wine. What shall I do?

Holding the vessel tightly to my bosom, I traveled far and wide, kissing the hands and touching the feet of the sages. But, dismayed, I returned unquenched. I was told that when you do not have an answer, Providence comes to your aid and responds, or sometimes the world answers your questions. But so far I have not received any solution for this unfathomable enigma.

I concluded that my thirst will be not quenched by the water of the streams, rivers, and fountains. I have an age-old thirst; I am an ancient drunkard. I have drunk the waters of these streams millions of times before, but still I find my thirst unquenched. I examined the beauty of the temporal and the mundane. It faded and never returned. Now the crying voice of my inner being coming from the depths of the vessel of life says, "Embrace me fearlessly. I will quench your thirst." Is it a deception, a hallucination, or a promise? I am still baffled, for I do not know how to approach the depths of my being. Darkness spreads Its veil before my eyes, and I am unable to see clearly.

For unveiling this truth, I need Thy help. Canst Thou illumine this tiny lamp with Thy magic touch, which will enable me to remove these barriers that separate me from Thee, though Thou art so near, so dear, seated in the depths of my being? And yet—I am lonely. My fingers are trembling with fear, for they do not have the capacity to tear the veil and reach Thee. Help, help, help me, my Love. For Thou hast always soothed my wounds and the inflictions I received from the cruel allurements of the world.

§

Eternal Communion

There came a time when my love wanted to find its way to fulfillment. A torn page of the manuscript of my life was brought forward by the stormy wind of time, but it could not be read, though the miracle creation of the ages was smiling on it.

Said She, "How tired and confused are you! Arise, awake, and gain knowledge. Do not act like a gigantic inert. Do not be a dumb and desolate one who knows not the meaning of life and its mysterious destiny. All human beings have essential potentialities to direct their lifestreams smoothly to the ocean of bliss.

"You have been graced to come to this world. Your chariot of life has come from a voyage unknown. What a fate! The day you are awakened to the fact that love is the creative principle of the universe, the divine mystery of existence that baffles all analysis, then you will be ashamed. Your soul will cry in bewilderment, but I will be not there to soothe you.

"Ye, listen to me. This procession of life is like a grand dance of stars in the infinite space, singing the song of the divine. You are marching toward ever unfolding potentialities of life, beyond the limitless horizon. Let us bathe together in the eternal light and be emancipated."

Unbelievably astonished, I said, "I have been waiting for ages for Thy glance and loving embrace. May I cross the mire of delusion? Let me soar high to the other shore of life, beyond time, space, and all bounds of the grand illusion. Let me unite and live in eternal joy. In every breath of my life there is the music of eternity, yet at times my human endeavor seems to become restless. Shall I light the fire and bathe in it? Then the whole will be revealed to me. It is not a mere subjective idea but an energizing truth. Dost Thou not see that deep in my heart Thy memory is treasured? Thy majestic beauty peeps through the little corridor of my life. My strength is Thy grace, which keeps this flame alive. I know that to receive eternal illumination, the veil of time, space, and causation needs to be lifted.

"Time, time, time has been the curse of my life and of many others. But in the depths of my heart dwells the eternal spirit of my love, which will one day transmute my whole being into the golden moments of joy. I have already made it clear that the architect of my philosophy of life is not the knowledge of the mind but a pure vision. Often my soul has experienced the Real and touched the Infinite. My restlessness is for Thy eternal communion."

§

My Love for Thee

Wisdom, intellect, and knowledge do not enrich my love for Thee. They remove me more and more from the intensity that I created with long hours of devotion and effort. Fused in love, I feel at home by rights of many births.

Said She, "I have noticed that you have only known the way of rationalization and intellectualization but not the way of receiving revelations, for this gift is not the product of mind but of intuition. Intellectualization is a sort of treachery in the interior world because it is mingled with doubt and prejudice, enveloped with profane and mundane longing."

I said, "I am not prepared to settle for less than the joy of the empyrean realm, for I have already examined the moments of the temporal. I know that words do not cook the rice. For cooking rice, first you have to light the fire; then you have to separate the rice from the husk. To quench the thirst, you have to separate the weed from the water. I am thirsty. Even if you pour seven seas of water into my mouth, it will not quench my thirst. No more water do I need to quench my thirst. I need a drop of nectar from Thy chalice so that my thirst is quenched and my dream of dreams is realized. My love for you is immense and enormous, unmeasured by logical standards. I know with all my certainty that Thou always dwellest in the inner chamber of my being."

Said She, "Do you know the finest and surest way of knowing? What obstructs your flow in allowing your spontaneity to proceed toward its destiny? Many a times we are born, and many a times we die. You have forgotten but not I. Do you believe in the great saying of the Bhagavad Gita? Krishna says to Arjuna, 'You know them not; I know them all.' This is in reference to the age-old link of love between the two, which they had shared many lifetimes. Arjuna forgot, and Krishna remembered. How unfortunate it is that one remembers but not the other. Does it not create a gulf? That is why this numerical space stands between the two."

§

Thou Art Inexplicable

To me, where this life ends, the mystery of love begins. Many births and deaths have I seen. I know them not; Thou knowest them all. Thy love has given me the correct perspective from which to perceive this world in the fullness of its beauty. And as I saw the picture of the universe against the background of Thy image, which I hold in my heart, I found it entrancing. I see an inevitable phase of life that gives me a vision of eternal joy. Yet I find myself in the depth of sweet sorrow. I do not know why.

Thou art exquisite beauty and a perennial flame of love. Art Thou not a wonder, a dream—an eternal dream of limitless joy? In the depths of my life, the eye of my heart sees the illumination of love. And from the depths of my being comes the music of silence, which echoes its mysterious movements, resounding in my ears as captivating song and melody.

Thus from the unity of space, my love finds its abode manifested in all things. Then I can tune myself to the harmony of the cosmos. But, O my sleepingly silent Love, Thou alone gavest me wisdom to see the unity in diversity through Thy rhythmic vibrations. Thus I began admiring beauty in its due place and realized that every movement and every sound that passes on to the finite space is in full accord with eternal law. Thou, my eternal Love, wilt never vanish from the inner chamber of my being.

One lonely morning came revelation, as the light with the dawn—and the pains and miseries of my life disappeared as darkness and mist when the sun rises. Lo! I found out that death itself is horrified to hold me in her bosom. I came back to fulfill my longing and was born many a time.

When the sun came out of its bed I was already awake. Last night for hours and hours together I peeked through my window and looked toward the sky. There I found stars hung on high pillars, whispering into the ears of heaven. Can my fingers reach there? The itching of the heart cannot be scratched. The mortal eye is not capable of seeing. Yet I know Thou art there. Thou art a self-existing reality.

When my whole being became an eye, I could see Thee. Thou wert the same light, my guide, my love, my life. I remembered that death has no power to change; that which has the power to change is called love. O my Love, dearer than my soul, I verily need nothing. I want to compose my inspirations and sing that eternal song which I breathe in every breath of my life. But I cannot sing Thy praises, for words are shallow. I find no means to explain Thy beauty.

§

Exalted Love

Love is the Lord of Life. Life without love is like an infertile, barren field. No matter how much it is tilled, nothing grows. The subtlest realm of love is unfathomable by those who live through their minds. A rare, fortunate few, those who truly learn to love, alone have access to this realm. In ancient times, the people of wisdom were aware of that.

The Absolute smiles through the human being. Those who have an eye to observe can see the Absolute in the human existence. Wise is he who knows that a human being is the shrine of the Lord, and the inner dweller in him is the Lord of Life and Love. Nothing can exist without the existence of the Absolute. Therefore, the Absolute is love eternal. Nothing can survive without love. Therefore, life is love. O Lord of Life, let this brooklet of life flow to the ocean of love. This little one has been rushing, and roaring, just to meet Thee.

True lovers understand that love for the objects of the world is very frail and fleeting, and it is fatal to depend on such a crutch which is constantly changing. The eternal alone can be loved with fulfillment, for the eternal alone is present here, there, and everywhere.

Love is the most ancient traveler, which engulfs the beauty of the universe and assumes its form. My exalted love finds its abode in one existence without a second. It is changeless, limitless, and eternal.

Love is giving, without expecting any reward. If there is total surrender to it, it showers happiness and bliss. It is beyond human expression and is therefore inexplicable, for you can feel, but cannot speak about it. Go from one end to the other end of the earth, learning all the languages and expressions of all human cultures, and you will find there is no word in any of the languages that can convey the true meaning of love. It is the language in which a newborn fawn speaks to her mother. It is a language of the heart that can be felt, but not painted on canvas. One can sing the songs of life, but the songs of true love are unsung. The day one awakens to the reality that he is a drop of the limitless ocean of love, his purpose of life is fulfilled. Having faith in God without love is revering a demigod in vain. One who does not see the Absolute in living creatures, but worships God only in the temple, is wasting his time in building a fool's paradise. The human shrine is the highest and most glorious.

Said She, "I am alone, but aloneness is not created by the absence of beings around me. It is created by my very nature, for I am closer to the Absolute One, and therefore I am a superior bright being, and no mortal being is able to unite with me."

Said I, "I have been repeatedly telling Thee that my love is an ancient traveler that will not stop unless it engulfs Thy beauty forever and ever. My exalted love I do not want to share with anyone but Thee alone."

§

Flow of Love

Today something strange came to my attention that made me wonder why I am writing this: someone silently whispered that you cannot do something for a long time if you are not meant to do it. I am habitually compelled to read and write and spend long hours drawing empty, dummy, and dark words. Will it be useful, or a mere pastime? Is it an amusement or a mission to be accomplished?

When I examined the long eventful chain of my unknown journey of life, I found out that every place I visited I did something useful and then went forward, forgetting what I had done before. Today I realize that activity in life sustains life on this plane. I have left everything to Providence, for Providence leads me to do that which is to be done.

When certain thoughts arise from their deep and long sleep in the bed of the unconscious, they agitate my conscious mind to do something untimely. I am at a loss to understand why these compelling charms are trying to deviate my attitudes away from my free thinking and living. Others may misconceive this as an exhibition of my irresponsibility, but I am sure that, like other events in my life, this is also something spontaneous coming to me from Providence.

Life is eventful. Some events can be analyzed, but not all. Why do we meet someone and get attached and think that this particular person is our friend and then start expecting impossible things? And if they do not get fulfilled, we cry with our impossible cries.

The child in the human never dies. He does not want to grow up, for he knows that in childhood he is unconditionally loved even by strangers. Perhaps this is the reason that every man on earth is still a child and hesitates in growing. The law of life is to leave behind the ground one is standing on and

31

then to step forward. This leads one to understand that he is the same, though on new soil.

Can anyone change? What could that change be? Writers and poets repeat one and the same thing. The flowers are the same, they only change the vases. What fun is there in knowing that which is already known? It is more interesting to stop the channel of thinking and start opening the gates of another avenue, through which flows the unalloyed knowledge of intuition that bypasses the perception of the senses and conception of the mind. It is pure, clean, ever green, ever fresh. It brings joy—an overwhelming feeling of the flow of love coming from eternity and flowing toward eternity. When this flow is hindered for a while, it creates a stagnant pool.

Therefore, let Thou flow Thy own way, O Love of love. I stand on the bank just witnessing Thy flow, waiting to receive Thy bountiful love. From eternity to eternity Thou flowest without any rest and repose.

§

Dialogue with the Stream

O fountain of the mountain, glory to thee! You are the greatest of all examples that I have before me. These ancient insurmountable mountains stand steady and still, perhaps contemplating the music played by you. You sing a song and continue singing it. In whose praise are these lyrics sung by you? You charm many other streams and assimilate them into your oneness.

I stand on the bank looking at your rushing waves and ripples. How strong and fearless thou art! You flow with your crashing roaring speed, dancing and singing the song of life. What a strange phenomenon I observe here. The water that passes by should create a gulf, but one wave of your waters is followed intimately by another, and here you establish the law that giving means receiving. You forsake your water, and you receive the same from your perennial springs. I do not ever find you empty. Who bestowed these graceful blessings upon you? You give away all the waters you have, and yet you are always full.

The stream said, "Do not forget that love is the law of giving. And when you have learned to love—to give—you receive."

This mutual exchange fulfills me. I am never lonely, for I am in love. One after another these waves are whispering their mute songs to me. I wish they could stay for a while and impart to me the profound secrets of their lyrics.

I asked, "The everlasting continuity that is seen in your waters is amazing and inexplicable. Where are you rushing to?"

"To meet my Beloved," said she.

"Talk to me and let me know why you are rushing with this speed. Wait a moment and converse with me," I said.

"The perennial flow of my waters knows not how to stop, for I have known only one way, and that is just to flow freely. Walk thy way, seeker," said she.

This conversation passed one night when the moon was paling its gentle light above, and below, the river was singing its song perennial. I was all alone, sitting and waiting for profound answers.

The life of this fountain begins from the heights of the mountain by creating music, as though a great orchestra were being played in honor of the perennial waters. Do you have an ear to hear this music?

Early in the morning, dawn started tearing the mist, and I rose and began walking all alone on the path.

§

Love Within and Without

When you cast off all the fetters of inconsistency and uncertainty, then alone do you grow into the spirit of limitless love. Then this inferior law of nature is replaced by the quest of love. There you experience a peculiar force in action, a divine knowledge resting in an unfathomable repose. Love finds its way to fulfillment if it is not haunted by desires and expectations.

But still there remains the question of transition; for there must be transition proceeding by steps, for nothing in the universe happens in an abrupt manner, without a clear procedure or basis. We have something we seek in us, and we have in practice to evolve out of this present situation.

Transition, therefore, is exceedingly important in the process of unfoldment. Not realizing the value of the present is ignorance mingled with inertness, a prime enemy of human unfoldment. It is a power of inaction, an obscurity that mistranslates anything into torpidity.

The joy of love is not a disintegration of energy or a vacant experience. It is an experience of the Eternal. Have you ever seen the Eternal sleeping? The Eternal does not need to sleep or rest; it does not get tired and flag. It has no need of a pause to refresh and recreate. It is not exhausted, for its energy is inexhaustibly the same, and infinite—like that of love. When worldly love is spiritualized—transformed from sense experience to soul experience—the values of life are understood. Love is always divine, one and the same, within and without both.

§

35

What Is Love?

Love in the mundane world is a pleasant, unforgettable memory of the glorious moments of the past. Therefore it should not be tormented by the shallowness of sounds and words. If it remains concealed, its revered memory lives fresh until the last breath of life. The quietest moments of my life were those when I conversed with Her unhesitatingly, without being aware of time, space, or anything that existed around me.

On this tree of life there are two fruits: one that sustains your life in this world, and another that leads you to the Divine. Though love for a human being is quite different from that for the Divine, if one knows how to expand human love, one catches a glimpse of the Divine. Verily, all love is one and the same: divine.

The fountainhead of life flows from the loving summit of divinity. It is a journey from the known to the unknown that makes me realize that to be in love is a part of worship and not of treachery. Yes, it is true that you love someone with your whole being but then become selfish in wanting to have everything from her. But that is not love at all.

The face of love glows with brilliance, like the dawn that tears the mist and gives free access to the blue and vast horizon. There in that infinite space are dancing billions of stars. They sing a mute song that is not comprehended by the human ear. The human ear has very little capacity to hear, but human eyes can peep and appreciate the twinkling lights of the stars and their subtle, rhythmic movements. For such a vision one has to make his entire being an eye, then he alone is a recipient.

Stars are beings like us. They shine with delight for us. Who bestows this light on them? The beloved Mother of this universe is self-illumined, a beauty who constantly radiates and flows forth as though there is an immanent message for us. Human endeavor and love for mortals are incomplete, for love for mortals separates one from the whole. Love for the form dissipates the mind, while love for the Infinite is not mere prevention of dissipation but total expansion in which lover and Beloved become inseparably one.

§

Melodies of My Life

When the great merciful Lord gave me the vision of the whole cosmos, I began composing the inspirations of my life in deep contemplation. These have enabled me to comprehend the profound meaning of life. Now I understand the mystery of the creation of the universe, its sublime simplicity and perfect lyric. Thou hast revealed to me all the divine movements beyond the forms and names of this world. Thus I could sing the songs that always bring the inner awakening that translates my past convictions into living truths.

But today my fingers are trembling and are unable to hold my pen. She is simply lame and mute. How can I draw my vision? She emphatically refuses me, saying, "Do not make an attempt; do not try." The compelling charm of this vision, due to its utter simplicity and fidelity, is overwhelmingly enormous. My pen says she can only draw the externals and line up in a row the empty words for miles and miles together, but cannot paint Thy glory. Is my vision delusion or truth?

Will there be a day when humanity realizes that the Infinite is seeking in the finite, and that perfect knowledge is seeking for love? When form and formless are united, love is fulfilled in devotion.

Thou seest me, Divinity, and I see Thee, and our love becomes mutual. How then canst Thou remain an unfathomable reality? Thou art within me. Thou art the magic stone that transmuted me by Thy touch. Thou art the builder and maker of my life. Thou hast laid the foundation stone of my philosophy of self-surrender. Thou hast introduced me to selfless service, self-surrender, and skillful action. Thou hast taught me not to realize my real Self through the hymns and songs of others. Yea, Thou art my eternal lotus and a dream of the limitless. Unveil Thyself, embrace me, my love. Why art Thou seated in the lonely corner of stagnation? Do not be a timid orthodoxy, and do not tease my imagination. My beliefs are well-filtered by time. My ideas have crossed beyond the golden angles of the sun, moon, and stars. The bird of my imagination has flown beyond the boundaries of all galaxies.

§

The Path of Love

Once upon a time I asked this question to my Lady of Love: "Tell me truly the path that is best for all mankind, that is based on truth, and that will lead the whole of humanity in order and justice, singing the song of the Divine and Perfect." This was the desire of desires that I had in my mind.

Across intervals of my silence, depression, and defeat, Thou hast guided me, a ray of hope that inspires me to live. Just last winter Thou gavest me a vision, and I heard a voice saying, "Light your lamp of love, and do not allow it to be diminished. See the light shining forth from within." The voice again proclaimed, "You are the ancient traveler, you are the magic-maker, you are the dreamer of dreams. Why do you not realize this truth of truths?"

I have contemplated on Thee in every breath of my life, so much that I forgot all the existence of my being. I continue to remember Thee while walking, standing, sitting, and lying down until sleep takes me to her sacred bosom. Thy memory has woven the fabric of my inner being. Now Thou sayest that I must turn the eyes of my crying spirit toward the abstract, the formless, beyond all objects and names.

I have learned to live for all these years with my eternal love. I worked hard, untiringly, day and night, not for my spiritual ecstasy, not to wash off the dark shadows of my lonely past, but for the spiritual emancipation of mankind. What happened to my vision of interpenetrating triangles signifying the penetration of the lower and the higher? The ascending and descending forces of life are trying to form uniformity. Ah, I find the same beauty and grandeur in the form and the formless, in the gross and the subtle, in the animate and the inanimate. One without a second enjoys its unfettered majesty.

I believe that I was sent to this world to whisper the gospel of love, for the gospel of truth has already been expounded a million times by many before. I am a messenger, a child of the Himalayan sages. I belong to all nations, and selfless service is the singular expression of my pure love. This is the fullness of life. It can only be reached by perfecting the relationship with the Self of all, with harmonious love given freely without any hesitation or reservation. Humanity will see that bright day only through love. It will attain the next step of civilization through the realization of divine love, that invisible motivating force that lights the lamp with its magic touch.

When it embraces the Lord of Love as the very basis of living and being, what will be the fate of the priesthood? Who will go pray in the temples and churches? There will be no multiplicity of shrines. Every human being's heart will become an altar of love. O Infinite Friend, O Love of Mankind, let Thou radiate Thy love and initiate the whole of humanity so that each person embraces all and excludes none.

O my fellow travelers, do not create a gulf anymore. Do not try to replenish yourself with mundane wealth, which can never fulfill. When you and I sit side by side you create a gap, a dangerous gulf, concealed under the glittering quicksand of the world. Wake up! You are still in the depths of sleep. You are captive in a solitary cage with no horizon beyond it. Come out of this imprisonment, for I am incomplete without you.

§

Love Is Deathless

Death, space, and time have so far been unsolvable riddles for many thinkers, but death has many times opened her golden vents for me to peep into the secret of eternal life. Do you mean to say that when you die you cease to live? That is absolutely incorrect. You live and live, for the life force is one, eternal, and all-pervading.

Death has for ages been the source of fear, misery, and pain because people have never pondered over the realities and travails of life. Oh! Ye who suffer and fear the approach of death should learn to hear the music of the eternal silence, where the Deathless resides in its timeless repose.

I have been waiting for that day when every man and woman will strive to secure the light of truth and live simply and wisely for the common good. There will be absolute freedom from the bondage of karma, and no one will suffer from the pangs and sorrows that are brought by the visit of death. One has simply to learn to tune the chords of one's being and make them move in harmony with the music of the cosmos. Then death will become the sweet music of a lullaby.

All existence constitutes the one organism of the entire cosmos, emanating love as the highest manifestation of its vital energy and having consciousness as the center of the spiritual galaxy. To comprehend this, the heart of man need simply be transformed to enable it to discover the harmaony in the universe. Then it will spontaneously attune itself to the music of all spheres and will find peace on this earth. I believe that man is still an unfinished being, but when love finds its abode in all things, then the discovery of love will lead him to its highest peaks, and the entire humanity will bind itself into a solid frame of joy, and man will be complete.

Through compasssion alone mankind will attain knowledge and wisdom to behold the light of truth, freedom, and happiness. Mere fancies, fantasies, and vain illusions will disapper. To learn this philosophy, one will have to become the student of life. Then philosophy will surmount all the obstacles, and the blessed one will ascend to the summit of the mountain of completion and perceive the grand vista of valleys and plains below. Then the purifying festival celebrated by merciful death will no longer remain a source of sorrowful misery. Joy, joy, joy! You will hear death whispering the secret of life here and hereafter.

The secrets of birth and death are revealed to the fortunate few only. Long are the arms that embrace the whole, the arms of love. Those who learn to love and live according to the law of self-surrender and giving know not the fear of death.

O man, you were never born, therefore you never die. The stream of life flows perennially from eternity to eternity. Those who believe in death suffer by the terrible fear created by the pangs of death.

§

Truth Weds Love

I was really baffled, for I found that truth came to me like a revelation of light in the darkness, and I was unable to share it with my fellowmen. Why has truth not been able to reach all the obscure corners of humanity? I see people all over the world blindly and fearfully following the path of lifeless formalism. And I know now that the revelation that brought the first glimpse of truth to me was without love. Now I understand that truth will shine its pure light through its inner realization, but only when mingled with compassion. Without love, truth and divinity are fantasies and wild exaggerations that will never be able to transform the human personality, and humanity will not be able to see the golden light of the dawn of a new civilization.

The truth that now fills my heart is deeply mingled with love, and now I am aware that they are inseparable twin laws of life. This realization has illumined my entire life. I have not received this wisdom from anyone: it came from within. After practicing truth with mind, action, and speech, I found that the little vessel of my being was still making noise, and I remembered the saying, "The empty vessel makes noise, but not the filled one."

When Thou didst fill my being, then O Adorable One, I accepted Thee as the supreme judge of my actions and speech and made the altar of my heart as Thy permanent abode.

Now my love finds its way to fulfillment. I realize that truth without love is a dormant fire deeply buried beneath the dense layer of the ashes of ignorance. O my crying soul, bathe in the light of love! Be eternal, my love, be eternal, be eternal.

§

The Purpose of Human Life

Love is the absolute Reality and the Lord of Life, as good is the reality of being. It is the essence of life and must be the principal object of realization for all.

This supreme love is the fountainhead of all the great teachings spoken throughout the ages by the enlightened and compassionate ones. Enveloped in the same consciousness, here I stand as Thy little instrument. Wilt Thou play through me? Play on this little instrument and create a melody that comforts the suffering humanity. Then the purpose of my life shall be fulfilled. All hatred, battles, and boundaries will be dead, and the flower of humanity will blossom. All the heavenly joys will be at the command of human beings. Concepts of heaven and hell will be washed away. Peace and happiness will prevail all around. There will be no desire for any heaven hereafter, for heaven will be established here and now. Is it not the Lord's earth? Is it not His beauty? Is it not His grandeur? Those who do not revere the Creator in His creation can never attain.

Today the world lives under the law of fear, trembling with doubts and uncertainty. I have met many leaders but have not encountered any prophet of the law of love. I have yet to meet that one who teaches selfless service, sympathy, and goodwill, and who identifies with the true happiness of others and the highest good of mankind.

O Dweller of Absolute Silence! Now Thou has started emanating forth into the future, blending Thy glory with the best that I have. Yes, I carry Thy sweet memories, which I cherish the most. They constantly ramble in the garden of my heart and the meadows of my conscousness. Certainly didst

Thou lift the veil of my consciousness and lead me to the summit of life. Lo! I hear the voice bidding me look into the hearts of my fellowmen and share with them the nectar given by Thee. Thou has taught me to live in sympathy with all that is beautiful and to love all that there is. Thou gavest me strength to step forth into the dense abodes of men, where sorrow is deep and ignorance is thick. Taking a little child by the hand, Thou didst ask me to leave the verdant aroma of the Himalayas, my garden of delight. What a daring adventure! Again Thy voice did lead me to go from land to land with searching eye and listening ear, to seek deeper knowledge. I journeyed and saw the curse of disparity and the darkness of prejudice, the blindness of hatred in which men live as strangers under the same roof. Yet I was still patient, and somewhere found the dynamic force of love hidden in humanity. The force that realizes the all-pervading one Reality will transform the whole of humanity and its habit of self-destruction into an exquisite piece of art. I am waiting patiently, but the bounds of patience are rushing to break.

Let me live my little days. I do not want to be any part of this society that remains under the law of contraction and knows not the law of expansion. Every individual is meant to radiate his love from individuality to universality. An individual is a nucleus and the universe is its expansion. Are they not qualitatively one and the same? When every human being lights his lamp, there will be illumination all around, and darkness will disapperar. Every human being will walk on light, and all miseries and pains will be annihilated. Then the whole universe will be one solid conglomerate, and the entire humanity will celebrate a grand festival. That will be the day when the purpose of human life will be fulfilled.

§

Conflict

A thought rolled down from the heights of my being and awakened me: "Time and traditions are your great enemies, for they are the strongest conditions of your mind." It was in the year 1952, when I revolted, renouncing the dignity and prestige that had been given to me as a gift. Then the ancient seeds of *samskaras** began sprouting with all their colors. They started growing their roots in the soil of my mind. These irrational repressions and accumulations of dead centuries began creating pain for me. I felt like a sluggish stream choked by rotting weeds. During those days my mind was obsessed by a desire that haunted me. My soul was shrunken in deep sorrow. My days were full of want and my nights laden with desire. I wondered how such an obsession could control my day-to-day life. I knew that I was on the verge of embracing something mundane. I tried to lift the veil of the future but could not. Something was deeply buried in the tomb of my heart.

This mundane desire wanted to change the course of my life. Its influence continued for many days. Then one day I dreamt that in the realm of faith for the Divine lies perfection, and I started examining the records of the greatest of ancient dreamers. I decided to follow the footprints of the elders who had already trodden the path. I studied the lives of the great designers of paradise, but without solution, and returned with utter disappointment.

The thought that brought me back to this mortal world is more powerful than the desire for self-enlightenment: "Why are the people of the world suffering from the sense of guilt,

---

*Subtle impressions of past actions.

a source of discord? Why is humanity caught in the snare of the fear of sinning? Why doesn't the flower of humanity bloom in its youthful vigor? Is it nature, God, or human beings who create suffering?"

"Thy knowledge is immeasurably immense," said I. "Why dost Thou not guide me at this hour of conflict and strife?"

Thus She spoke, "When a human being forgets his essential nature and identifies himself with the temporal and perishable, he becomes miserable. Miserable is he who forgets his own real Self. Can there be a greater saying than this? The greatest of all sins is to kill one's own conscience and persist in doing so. Sinning affects the mental life of a man who is weak and frail. Prayer and repentance purify the way of the soul, and Self-realization leads him to the goal."

§

Beyond Religion

I do not believe in any religion, for they seem too petty, bound with blind regulations of no essential observance. No religion shows the path of truth, the path of freedom. They create fear that invites danger. Thus liberation remains an unrealized dream. What good are these blind injunctions and laws enveloped by fears, selfishness, egotism, pride, and prejudices? Why this multiplicity of shrines, which dissipates the single-pointedness of humanity and robs its chastity, purity, and divine love?

There is something beyond religion. Religion is an act that is man's relationship with God. It is essential in the preliminary stage but surely does not allow one to be one with the whole. God's existence in reality does not depend on our proofs. There is something untidy in the thinking of theologians, for they have the curious notion that God is a kind of hypothesis that can be analyzed and discussed. Everywhere in the realm of religion I encountered locked doors. If ever a door should chance to open, I was disappointed by what lay behind it. Religion is man-made, and only a preparation for attaining the Divine.

§

Living Beauty

What beauty and grandeur a flower bestows! The naive take this lightly and are not sensitive enough to perceive the depth of the colors of the delicate petals.

For a short while the flower blooms, and then the petals drop to the dust without receiving any admiration or touch of love. Do you know, they cry for want of love, and that is why they are shy and drop their blossoms unnoticed in quiet lonely nights.

A flower is a living beauty that blooms only once and vanishes forever. It whispers vainly—for the deaf ears of the cruel human being have no power to listen to that pain. The flower waits to offer its petals to her Beloved before the dust assimilates her beauty and blends it into its gray ugly color.

Who has such an intense feeling of sensitivity to communicate with the blessed flower, which knows nothing but gives unconditionally and without reservation?

One day a priest gripped the stem of a flower, wanting to have it for his altar. While carrying that flower, he stumbled, and the flower said, "O priest, are you injured?" Hearing the whispering voice of the flower, the priest wept. He felt as though he had twisted the neck of his own infant and was going to offer it to the dumb, lifeless image that was installed on the altar. Whenever one approaches the altar, that image never speaks or moves. What good is this worship for which the tender infant of nature is snatched from its mother and offered to an inert, dumb god? Afflicted by the crying voice of the flower, the priest abandoned worship and from that day lived in solitude, contemplating the formless and limitless Infinity.

Human beings have strange and inauspicious methods of worship that have no purity, sincerity, or validity.

§

Misery Is Self-Created

Life is eventfully mysterious and eventually joyous. In life there come many moments of inner uncertainty when the decisive faculty takes off and does not know where to land. It is a state of disorientation in which one feels totally suspended in midair until he finds a landing place where he can have firm footing.

Life proves itself to him who has a sense of destiny. It is assigned by fate. Fate is a creation of one's past deeds. There is no choice but to fulfill it. Parched and weary, I started believing that life is not a mere chance or accident, but that enjoined upon me is what Providence wants and not what I want. Indeed, when no one is able to rob this conviction, then one attains a state of equanimity, equilibrium, and tranquility.

Many a time I had the feeling that in all the decisive matters, I was no longer among my fellowmen but together with some higher power. I was not lonely, for I was no longer alone. I was beyond time. I felt that I was an ancient traveler and belonged to the centuries.

Sometimes, for lack of a solution, uncertainty stunned me, and then I took refuge in silence, working to receive guidance from my Beloved, beyond the mire of delusion. Silence led me beyond the bounds of my thinking process. I forgot all the languages I knew. I did not know how to think. Then, by the grace of my Beloved, the infinite library of intuition opened its brilliant gates to me.

Whenever I desired human help I found it futile and disappointing. Everyone's life seems to be surrounded by suffering, pain, and sorrow. Fear of losing and not gaining is an obsession of the human mind.

Parting from the objects of attachment makes one painfully

sad, and ignorance is the mother of all miseries. Perhaps people suffer because they do not admit the existence of death and change in life, and they struggle throughout because of this ignorance. Finally, all miseries are created by oneself, and are dispelled by the Self alone.

§

Emancipation

O expectation of my life, will you take off and never return again! You are the mother of all miseries. You prevent me from chanting the hymns of the Infinite; you prevent me from singing the gliding songs of my life. Interfere no more! What do you expect of me? The best of the moments of my life have evaporated into empty space, and the rest that I have is the dead weight of your meddling. Renunciate I am, but it is hard to renounce you. Wherever I venture, you follow me like my shadow, trying to deviate me from my path.

Great heroes, singers, poets, and writers, all became your victims. Have you spared no one? Expectation, do not lead me toward your blind destiny. You lure your prey with hope, promising to fulfill their deepest unthought dreams. But when they at last awaken to your treachery, they have lost both dream and reality, and their time is spent. O cruel temptress of humanity, I am aware of your evil skill in weaving subtle traps that sap the precious life force of a man. Do not make me your slave. Ye expectation, I proclaim emancipation from you!

§

A Vision in the Alps

Let me dwell for a moment longer on those early days when I had left my Himalayan abode and had just arrived in the deep recesses of the Alps. There arose from the bed of memory an ancient thought, unbelievable, high, and mighty. During that moment of spiritual vision an illumination of loving thoughts and conversations came clearly before me.

One evening the moon had just begun to rise, and the air was full of enchantment. Darkness was slowly creeping over the earth, and a beautiful afterglow of light was still visible in the West. The glamour of it all was upon me, and I wandered upon the mountain up and down, hardly knowing where I was going. At that hour I was literally oblivious to time, space, and things external. Then a wave of bliss arose in the sacred ocean of my heart. It crossed the bounds of individuality. My lips stuttered and could not mutter a word, for they could not capture the experience. I searched and searched the infinite library of my intuition and learning, but words were shallow and could not carry the weight of that vision. Then tears started rolling down on my tender cheeks. My mind rambled, my thoughts bewildered, and that dream suddenly vanished.

This was an inner vision of beauty that I saw with the eye of my being. It went far beyond the bounds of the temporal and mundane. That joy of illumination has never altogether passed away. I can never forget that vision; that memory unfailingly comes to me.

O Beloved, Thou hast introduced me to the secret of a new spirit of beauty in the universe. Since that day I have tried to see that beauty with my eyes, and to describe it through the song of my life as I build up its living fabric in my tender heart.

Anyone who knew my life before could appreciate how the

dividing line actually came here. What followed that moment has brought something new that has changed my whole outlook. That memory broke through the dull routine of outward form that had imprisoned me up to that time, and thus set me free.

Thou alone gavest me a gift of light—the fearless love of freedom and passionate devotion to truth—and the most daring adventure of my life. Then I learned the secret of perpetual youth. Since that day I have retained the heart of a child and kept the eager outlook of a new hope for a future filled with admiration and love.

Suffering can come to me in incredible forms of pain, and has awakened me from my sacred dreams. No one has suffered more acutely and sensitively than have I. It is Thy love—ever new, ever young, ever fresh, with the fullness of new life and tender with the wisdom of sorrow—that has continually won my heart and quickened my inner spirit. In the untarnished mirror of my own innocent and childlike heart, Thy vision is still reflected. Again I hear the soft voice rising and falling, its surging inward emotion plaintively crying, "Save me, save me, my Love, save me."

§

From the Bed of Memory

Suddenly a fragment of memory rolled down from the deeper recesses of my being. It unbelievably forced itself forward from the forgotten past. I felt profoundly overwhelmed by this experience. Emotions are as ancient as the sky, streams, mountains, fruits, and flowers. It awakened me and whispered that secret into my ears which I am not prepared to part with, for fear that such experiences could be misunderstood. At that moment of awakening I was oblivious to time and space. Not until the next day did I understand the meaning of this vision, which was a pure gift of Providence. Why did I not have it before? That was too much for me to expect. Believe me or not, there was no effort on my part to recall this deeply embedded memory. There seems to be unlimited knowledge in the infinite library stored within us. It is not comprehended through the mind but is known only through the way of intuition, and only when the time is ripe. Can you believe that sometimes the dead and buried past can answer a crucial question?

Many times when I cannot solve an intricate riddle, the unconscious helps me to solve it. It has an entirely different way of informing me of that which, by all logic, I could not possibly know. Whenever I tried to share these experiences with someone, he mistrusted me, which crippled and injured the delicacy of the unexplainable phenomenon and gave me pain. I feel that rationalism, dogmatism, and doctrinism are limiting barriers that prevent the spontaneity of the flow of intuition.

In this very birth we can know that we have been experiencing two lives: the one we live and the one that is forgotten. What has been apparently lost does not come to the fore again without sufficient reason. When the occasion arises, the forgotten comes forward with all its spontaneity. In the living structure of our lives, nothing takes place in a merely mechanical fashion. Everything fits in the economy of the whole, relates to the whole. Everything is purposeful and has a profound meaning. But the conscious part of the mind is unable to comprehend the view of the whole. It usually cannot grasp the meaning and purpose of the past impressions that often haunt our thinking process.

We must therefore content ourselves with nothing, and accept the phenomenon with the contention and hope that the future will reveal the truth. Do you have the patience to wait? I have not. In any case, I did not ever have even a glimmering of such an experience before. Now the experience lingers in the bed of my memory all the time, along with the loveliest wish to have a glimpse of that vision again. But that wish totally depends on fate, which still lies in the womb of the invisible future. Sometimes one never knows which is more enjoyable—catching sight of the new, or discovering new approaches to the age-old, which is preserved in the treasury of the golden past. The wheel of life rotates mysteriously.

When I opened my eyes to external reality, I saw the mountain in front of me fully enveloped by the folds of clouds, and my memory disappeared to perform its mysterious duty. I am not permitted to name the name of the beauty who gave me that vision. This is not, I feel, mystification but a vital mystery whose betrayal might bring about the downfall of my thoughts, words, and inspirations. This exquisite mystery will continue to exist as long as it remains concealed.

It is astonishing to me to see how solitude brings forth something enormously precious and meaningful from the buried records of the past. Ordinarily, such experiences do not occur. They show a high degree of self-control and dignity.

My memories are not theories to me. They are as real as

present occurrences. When insoluble riddles present themselves to me, I start crying, and then go to deep silence, because silence alone offers all the answers I need.

Now the blazing sun is rising higher and higher. My excitement, which was already perceptible, mounts to greater heights. There is nothing to say now. I have come to the peak of an insurmountable summit.

§

Transformation

I was tired and weary, and fell asleep in my armchair. My sleep lasted until midnight, when my dream awoke me and I found myself transformed and transported to a different realm. Sometimes I touch the state of ecstasy and during that time I float effortlessly and go towards the void with the deepest feeling of happiness and joy. I have seen all the wonders of the world, but this experience was so strangely wonderful that it is beyond my description.

This experience brought me to the awareness that dreams can reveal something unique that cannot be known during the waking state. In Sanskrit such a state is called "unmani." There is no equivalent of this word in English, therefore I call it a dream. It is an intermediate state between waking and sleeping.

I am being enigmatic in saying that I am one of the greatest dreamers, but in reality I do not dream at all. My sleep takes me to a realm and depth in which the contents of mind are absent. In reality I have no time to dream. There are moments before I go to the deep state of sleepless sleep, in which I remain fully awake, where I find myself on a summit looking down into the valleys all around. During this time my past, present, and future are clearly seen. Yet I remain in an entirely different state, which is neither waking, dreaming, nor sleeping. Indeed, it is glorious. Time, space, and causality are conditionings of that mind which remains bound by selfish, mundane motivations, clinging to the glittering objects and forms of the world. That is a sense-created reality.

"There are many such realms that are created by the clouded mind, causing congestion for the intellect. It is said that one is real and another is not, but in reality everything is real, and the unreal is experienced when we compare the two realities without examining their very basis.

"There is only one truth, and therefore only one reality, though on various degrees and grades. Nothing is new, nothing is old, and everything is in the eternal. You and I are looking toward the horizon from different perspectives, and that is why the reality of vision seems to differ. When one tunes to the dimension of another's reality, there exists only one whole. One alone exists, and all that exists is but the manifestation of the same One that existed before. There is nothing new. Apparent newness is an amusement of sense perception. But when you transport yourself into the delight of the Absolute, there you find all thoughts and feelings blending into one colorless color. Actually there is only one color, and all colors are but its variations.

"Confusion proceeds because of multiplicity. Between one and two lies a space that distinguishes the same self-existent One in a different way. Manyness is one of the conditionings of the human mind. Multiplicity proves the validity of one-ness, just as shadow proves the validity of light. Inseparably one they are. In the sphere of inseparable unity there is no discontinuity.

"Intellectualizing is like creating a new reality by losing touch with the real. There is another way of experiencing the Reality that is not subject to change in the past, present, or future. When the individual self surrenders itself to the cosmic One, like a drop of water to the ocean, then individuality finds its way to perfection, as a stream to the boundless sea.

"Only a fortunate few have touched this Reality, for which there is no name. It is beyond all explanation—and is subject only to that incredible experience that has no tongue. When one learns to forget all that one remembers, then in which language will the mind think? The thinker has nothing to think upon. Therefore, there is no thought and no mind.

Only the Self exists with its majestic glory, which is simply beautiful and indescribable. It is an experience that elevates one to the height of completion and fearlessness, for there is nothing that is able to create fear. The One exists alone in its entirety."

§

Time Beyond Time

Last night I had a unique experience, neither pleasant nor unpleasant, but simply unusual. I did not have enough rest in the daytime, for I did not have time to recline. When this occurs, then during the early morning hours I take conscious rest and go to a state that I term sleepless sleep. This is a special gift I have received after long hours of contemplation and study of the three states of mind—waking, dreaming, and sleeping—with the determination to go beyond and then have the infinite view of all these three states in one glance.

I have never believed that someone could suddenly slice this state and wake me from this void. It happened last night. I concluded in the morning that it happened because of the strong ties and bonds I have with a bright being in the far distance, and perhaps Her immense desire to teach me was carried by the force of love and traveled to the end of this earth.

Love knows not time, for it is timeless. It alone is capable of removing the conditionings of time, space, and causation, and it can bring past and future into the presence of now. The unconscious is a vast reservoir of knowledge that can easily connect the missing links between the past, present, and future. I was consciously in the unconscious, like a tender child sleeping in the lap of the mother. The Mother Divine gave a tap of love upon my head and awakened me. I have a vivid idea that my Love of love wanted to give me a vision. That could be the only explanation. I leave it to fate to solve this riddle.

Sometimes the future tells the tale which remains untold, and sometimes the past also answers the questions that the present and future cannot. These three realities, past, present, and future, are like three distinct colors that make the painting of life exquisite. Who is this painter? You are the painter, the surveyor, the redeemer, and the dreamer of your dreams. If you can gather together past memories and future imaginations and bring them to the here and now, all the mysteries of life that are veiled in the past and all that is hidden in the womb of the future will be revealed to you here and now.

§

Unresolved Mystery

I met a potter who, while singing a song of his pride and valor, was a bit careless and a bit cruel in wedging the clay for his wheel. I heard the clay crying plaintively, "Gently, gently, be gentle. Put me on thy wheel." The potter did not care to listen to the cry of the clay and modeled it in his own way.

Human existence seems to be exactly like that. Arising from the dust and falling back to the dust again is the hopelessly pathetic history of human life. Someone unseen seems to shape the dust, gives it a form, and that form for a while moves. Finally, form disappears, and that self-existent force alone exists. This mystery has been baffling the intelligentsia throughout the ages, and so far the riddle remains unsolved.

Why do we come to this world, and where do we go from here? This issue poses a big question in the minds of thinkers. Great men say that it is a free play of the creator of this universe, exactly the way a potter shapes the clay according to his own whim. Does a human being have free will, or is it the will of Providence? Psychologists and philosophers differ in their opinions in answering this question.

The voice that speaks to me says, "Take life lightly, and do your duties seriously." The mystery of birth and death is still a mystery resolved by only a fortunate few.

§

The Preaching
of the Plants

The world of plants preaches a unique gospel. It expresses not only the beauty but the thoughts of God's creation, with no intent of its own, and without deviation. Trees in particular are mysterious and seem to me to be direct embodiments of the incomprehensible meaning of life. In the woods I feel close to my inner self, and the deepest meaning is revealed with its awe-inspiring workings. Down below when I look at the rocks, they impose an impression and enforce upon me an idea of the infinity of the cosmos. They spontaneously permit me to peep into the secrets of the universe, which helps to reveal the secrets of the whole.

Whenever I cannot judge the meaning and meaninglessness of impersonal purpose and mechanical law, which are both wrapped in the kingdom of rocks, I dimly feel my kinship, and with a little bit of effort it gives me joy to know the divine nature in both the dead and the living matter.

Sometimes I feel with all my being as though a breath of the infinite world of stars and endless space had touched me. When I bathe in sunlight with the winds and clouds moving over me, my being becomes exalted. When the gentle rain comes down with its rhythmic music, I feel as though thundering clouds were trumpeting the drums of delight. The soft green and fragrant winds are eagerly waiting to make an aristocrat of my life, forgetting that I am a traveler on the path of light. It is wonderful to be unsystematic with intention, to be like an irresponsible boy jumping in joy, playing with toys, and then resting in the lap of mother nature, where there are no dreams.

§

Just for Thee

Meaninglessness inhibits the fullness of life and is therefore equivalent to sickness. But meaningfulness gives one hope to live and love on this earth. How can one possibly live fully without comprehending the meaning of life, for life without love would be an utterly vacant experience. Scientific conclusions and logic can never replace love, no matter how lofty and high they are. This is my discovery. I borrowed it from no one; it was already there. My love is the revelation of the Divinity in me. How could it be ascribed to hallucination? One suffers because he becomes a victim of profound uncertainty that leads the mind to a state of bewilderment. Certainty is a part of free thinking and decisiveness, from which springs exquisite melodies.

The music that I compose is just for Thee, and the melody that I create is for Thee, and for no one else. When my song is exhausted, then I go to the deep recesses of silence in order to compose another song for Thee alone. Now the meaninglessness has disappeared, and I am a singer composing and singing Thy song in every breath of my life, just for Thee. I am Thine; Thou art mine.

§

To the Mother

I sing my songs by myself.
I find need for no one to sing them for me.
My songs are filled with delights; they are never empty
    or vacant.
They are hymns of the Mother Divine.
She is the beloved Mother of all.

How magnificent, wonderful, and grand Thou art!
To see Thy luminous face is the only desire I hold.
What a fate and destiny I have: Thou caresseth me, and I am
    unable to see Thee.
Surely, most certainly, one day I will see Thy face, in this
    lifetime, certainly.

How is it I am unable to see the face of my Mother?
I have been crying for ages, and Thou hast been wiping
    my tears.
The tears that moisten my eyelids make my vision blurred;
    everything looks hazy here and everywhere.
Give me vision, give me strength, and help me sing my
    infant song.

§

Thy Eternal Name

Oh, let me eternally breathe Thy name,
With the promise that I will till the last breath of my life.
Let me breathe Thy eternal name,
Thou who art splendid, formless, and nameless,
Thou who art the benevolent Mother.
O Thou—tenderness, sweetness, and pleasure—
Let me eternally breathe Thy name.
Thou—summits and thrilled vastness,
Transcendent, eternal bliss—
Let me breathe Thy eternal name.
O immutable, immovable, and imperishable Mother,
Immeasurable joy, limitless and infinite,
Let me eternally breathe Thy name.
Though Thou art nameless,
Yet Thou hast countless names.
I call Thee by a special name,
As an infant calls its mother.
May I pray Thy eternal prayer
And remember Thy name
Till the last breath of my life.

§

Above the Shore of Life

In the mountain by the shore of life
That thunders night and morn with human strife,
Sung to by that rude relentless sound,
Amid the howl of wind, a hallowed cave I found.

In joy went I to Himalaya's peak,
And on the highest heard the voice of wisdom speak.
In the breathless snow set down for many years,
Knowledge rushed streaming from the ancient seers.

A sudden silence and a sudden voice—
The voice above and from another world;
The silence here—and from the two unfurled
Resplendent brilliance—rejoice!

The valley shook echoes of descending power
And sent forth knowledge from that wondrous hour.
Of dumb silence have I tired;
From profounder night I come inspired!

Not sound nor silence, neither world nor void,
But unthinkable, absolute, unalloyed—
One voluminous, nameless yet with name,
Innumerably varied, yet eternally same.

§

Ye Dweller of the Silence

In deep silence of the night,
  In the still and gentle eve,
When the thought is plunged in loving
  Memories it cannot leave,

When dawn brings sudden light
  Across the clouded sky,
And the drizzling rain is sobbing,
  And breeze embraces in reply,

Smiles always Her face before me,
  And Her voice sings in my ear,
Enchanting, beautiful, ever gentle,
  With azure eyes austere.

Vapory figure, radiant, luminous
  With the life and light within,
When the soul came rippling outward,
  Did Thy awesome dance begin.

Cast to me, O Thou Beloved,
  A nod, a glance, a loving smile.
Release from me this malignant mood,
  And afflictions reconcile.

§

Mystic Miracle

By Thy grace Thou soarest high,
    And from Thy vantage flows
Both divinity and mortality.

Below expands disparity—
    Poverty, prosperity;
Fear and felicity.

Hold me in Thy sacred bosom
    With no more delay.
Bestow Thy grace, ye Eternal Blossom,
    Keep me not away!

All Thy gifts and bliss Thou unloose,
    All Thy pain and sorrow,
Even deadly hemlock juice
    Is welcome—morn, eve, or morrow.

Should my hand have to raise
    In Thy prayer or silent praise?
For Thou art mine,
    And I am Thine.

§

Sacred Fire

I have gathered my precious moments
  From the present and the golden past,
Preserving them gently within my heart,
  With the promise to eternally last.

I have been digging deep and long,
  To fulfill my inner desire:
A temple for the golden song,
  A shrine for the sacred fire.

I have labored day and night,
  To bring this fire to man;
But the fury of human spite
  Shatters the sacred plan.

I light my lamp of hope
  To lead me beyond the known,
And a guiding voice comes to me
  From the realm unknown.

My chanting hymns to the Beloved One
  Will be ceaselessly sung till my task is done.
Both men and angels mock and smile;
  My sorrow they never reconcile.

I dug deeper and deep again,
  But left disappointed and in vain.
Weary and tired I became,
  Knocking upon Thy gate again.

Suddenly a smile gleamed in the sky,
   Whispering songs of delight.
My crying spirit began soaring high
   To be blessed by Thy wondrous sight.

§

Death Is Life Disguised

Death is a prelude, a major change,
A habit of the body, preparation for the wedding day.
It is a span of joy in disguise.
It is a festival celebrated by the spirit on the other shore of life,
Where the spirit rejoices, shedding all the fetters of this life.
Darling Beloved, extend Thy loving hands;
Embrace me with Thy eternal arms.

Seer, O seer, stop for a moment;
Whisper thy secret with kind intent.
Are we only like seasonal flowers,
Or the travelers of endless hours?
"You are like the eternal lotus that untouched remains
During the heavy shower of torrential rains."

§

The Path of Light

Tell me about what the scriptures say—the secrets of the
   beginning and the end.

Said She, "These endless talks of the timeless rob the time
   of your little days.
They speak either of the bygone or the time to come,
   but nothing of here and now.
For me there never existed anything before now, nor will
   anything ever exist after now.
That which has always existed, exists now.

Everything is annihilated by the cruel laws of the past—
   no childhood, no youth exist, only faint memories.
The past is engulfed by darkness, and the future is not yet lit.
There is no perfection anywhere other than what exists now—
   neither concepts of hell nor heaven exist—
   perfection exists here and now.
Cry not; flow not the tears of sorrow; unlearn whatever you
   have learned; learn to be here and now.
Eternity is another name for now.
If you can extend now throughout eternity, it is surely here
   and now."

Does wisdom belong to past or future, or is it timeless and
   limitless? If it is true, then it must exist here and now.

Said She, "Eternity remains hidden from mortal beings all
   the time.
Pain lives in the memory of the past, in the hope of the future,
   and in the heart of want and desire.

Nature creates dissipation by scattering lustful charms with wild extravagance.

Pure and sweet is the soul filled with happiness, peace, and bliss—not of past nor future nor beyond, but of the self-existent Reality that is here and now.

Unseen and seen both dwell in the bosom of here and now.

The present is still, the past is quiet, the future is dim.

"I am an ancient traveler on the path of the unknown, but on my way awhile I repose.

Harboring glad and sublime,

Having lost the value of time,

All is beautiful, wonderful, and inexplicable.

Do you hear the sighs of rains and winds, the songs of birds and hums of bees?

These whispers are compelling and say, 'Delay no more, awake, arise.'

Rest is an invigorating prelude to walking on the light.

Wake up and tread thy path of light!"

§

To Time

Said She, "If your trembling fingers cannot lift the veil of the past, nor your eyes penetrate its deeper folds, you can still hear vividly the music of yesterday and distinguish my song being played on the strings of the void. My very dear one, know that time is the greatest healer and filter; it is a crude annihilator, which knows no forgiveness. It is time that has absorbed even the greatest prophets of all ages."

Below the peak of mountain,
The dead leaves fall and fall.
Drowned in the ancient fountain,
They drift beyond recall.

The stones, streams, and time have their existence,
But in them dwells no sense,
Dumb in their bonds and breathless,
Blind in their providence.

All things living and mortal
Are conditioned by time.
Time is a blind condition
Of the human mind.

§

Perpetual Youth

A yogi does not measure his life by the years but by the
  breaths he takes.
To say that he is old is an impossibility and a joke.
Old age is a mere reflection of the mind, and not of years.
Weakness and decrepitude creep in for lack of trust in truth,
  in justice, in oneself, or in one's kinsmen.

These are the signs of old age:
As soon as freshness and interest is gone out of one's life,
  he is old.
When one talks about killing time, he is becoming old.
He who is interested in nothing new is old.
He who is timid and afraid to undertake new enterprises
  is old.
One who has no self-reliance is old.
One who repeatedly cries for help is old.
The habitual fault-finder and complainer is old.
One who values mundane wealth more than uplifting
  thoughts is old.
One who clings to life and does not let go is old.
He who does not enjoy humor and has lost his smile is old.
One who does not enjoy laughter is old.
One who does not enjoy the song of the birds or the beauty
  of a flower is old.
One who has no control over his limbs and is horrified of
  death is old.
One who does not enjoy stillness, quietness, and silence
  is old.
One whose mind is like a crowded abode full of strife and
  misery is old.

But one who remains in the garden of delight and smiles
   perpetually is young.
One whose heart is ever fresh, ever green, is ever young.
Even if he has lived for many years, he is better than
   anyone young.

But why contrast these two, young and old, for both are
childlike. The difference is that in old age the mind remains
preoccupied with haunting memories of the past and is full of
follies, while at a young age the mind remains preoccupied
with curiosities and uncertainties. In old age the mind has had
all the experiences. It still has desires that wander into the
grooves of old habits, but the body does not follow. At a
young age one lacks experience, and wild ambitions try to
probe into the heights and depths of doubts and fears, wanting to gain new experiences. They give one zeal and hope,
but, still inexperienced, he stumbles many a time, hurting,
being hurt, always unsatisfied. This hope of expectation keeps
him seeking. The young person who lacks will, confidence,
hope, and wisdom is not able to accomplish what he wants.
In old age the charms have lost their allure, hopes are gone,
the experiences are completed. There is nothing new to be
relished.

The old man who keeps up his spirits and develops the art
of appreciating and admiring the beautiful is a beautiful old
man. He is better than any young person. There are many
young people who are like old people, and there are many old
people who retain their perpetual youth and remain young.

Someone once said to his beloved, "Old age is a matter of
mind—if you don't mind, it doesn't matter." O old man, keep
up your spirits, don't be lonely. Don't ever think that you are
old, for thinking makes it so.

§

Echoes of Life

Endeavor helps me have an eye
That cannot choose but see.
Seeking Thy blessed grace, I
Fused in love with Thee.

§

From the darkness of stormy night
The day breaks with the hope of light,
Bringing immense joy and gentle delights,
Leading to green valleys and majestic heights.

§

In twilight sky the stars light their lamps,
Shedding their bright and soothing light
Upon weary pilgrims' caravans and camps.
How auspicious it is when day weds the night!

§

Under the shade of the tree of life,
Seekers find rest and shelter from strife.
But the fruits of the tree are for the Lord alone,
And guidance by the radiant light is shown.

§

Some are great, some are glad.
Some are mute, some are sad.
The procession of life can distract and enthrall—
Unaffected and detached, I witness it all.

§

I make my heart an altar:
All the delights of my feelings,
All the petals of my speech,
All the fruits of my actions,
I offer to Thee, and I am free—emancipated!

§

The Way of Providence

There are three streams through which wisdom flows:
Firm faith in your highest Self, the teachings that are
filtered through a pure heart and mind, and the voice of
the clear conscience.

When decision is difficult or impossible, then go into the
mountain solitude, or into the retreat of your soul, or
await the word of Providence.

Accept not hastily all voices, for they may be waiting to rob
your faith. Let your heart be pure and your mind intent,
and then follow the way of Providence.

All wise thoughts and words proceed from the silence
of Infinity.
He who would attain the Divinity must endure endless trials,
but most seekers are eager instead to offer bribes.
As the bee suckles the nectar of the flowers, so the seeker
gathers twigs for the sacred fire.

§

The Self of All

No god is greater than the Self.
Therefore, O man, be not curious about God.
To hear and behold God in every object is mere knowledge,
  but to realize the Self within is real wisdom.
Who can there be more wonderful than the Self, who is the
  Self of all?
One who is without awareness of the Self walks to his own
  funeral.
It is a vain attempt to search for God.
When you see the same Self smiling through the faces of men,
  women, and children, then for whom are you seeking?
Why then should one crave to see God?
When I hear the whispers of the stars in heaven, the songs
  of the streams, the silence of the mountains, and the
  trumpeting of the ocean, I rejoice in gladness that all
  is for me.
I know not the name of the nameless, and am sure no one has
  ever known.
The ancients tried, and even some modern ones impose
  countless names, but it is still a word unheard, unknown,
  and unsaid—everlasting, constantly moving, yet motionless.
Is it happiness, wonder, or an eternal whisper, inexplicable?

Many a time, I filled and emptied the vessels of my past and
  future, emptied and filled them again and again.
I have been born a million times and died a million times, too.
Oh, death and birth are festivities I have celebrated countless
  times.
For, could there be anything more glorious to celebrate
  than this?
I proceed to unveil the mysteries of my future.

I said to Her, "Listen to my cry—talk to me directly, look at
   my face.
Wrenched and sweaty, parched, exhausted am I.
Will you whisper clearly, nay, talk to me directly, before I am
gone, my Love?"

§

Blossoms Dropped by the Night

What do you do?

I pick up the blossoms dropped by night,
I listen to the whispers of silence.
I contemplate on the vast void within.
I babble Her name in each breath of my life.
I revere the beauty of Her radiant face.

When sun comes out of bed, I retire.
I enter the depths of void and bathe in the eternal fire.
Through the clouds of joy,
The wingless bird of my spirit soars higher and higher.
I am in love and fused beyond desire.

That is what I do.

§

Hermitage in the Mountains

If choose I might a dwelling place,
A calm abode without travail,
I choose a hermitage of sublime grace
On a mountain by a vale.

To see heaven on earth here and now
With the efforts life can allow—
Do I need a friend or roof,
Silken array or weatherproof?

I ask not solace from human soul,
From relative, neighbor, or friend.
My life's purpose has a splendid goal:
Thou alone to comprehend.

Neither child nor maid do I require,
No rooms full of eyes that could but admire.
Deep in joy and fused with love,
Infinity surrounds me below and above.

I ask for neither name nor fame
Nor blustery trumpeting.
Casting off both sigh and shame—
Woman and wealth—to nothing I cling!

But on my mountain,
lightly My heart may complete at ease
Life's deep desiring for the deep,
Mingled with mountain memories.

And my own rivulet of rhyme
May run from summit to the sea,
Singing along the edge of life
The music of eternity.

§

To and Fro

I am only a narrator and not even a perfect one. I narrate only that which I receive. My stories will be narrated till they are completely exhausted. They seem to be endless.

All unions finally are united in the Absolute. What difference does it make to me if Thou keepest Thyself quite aloof, if Thou, who art my Love of love and darling dearer than my soul, create an infinite space between Thee and me?

But this is simply intolerable. It plunges me into the sea of sorrow. Thou who hast profound knowledge of the whole in its entirety still controllest my emotional life, exactly as a mother does her child's. My tender mind is constantly haunted by Thy presence to and fro.

§

Vagabond

The greatest wisdom that ever I have heard is when Thou didst whisper into my ear the secret of my folly. In vain I was roaming here and there, journeying far and wide, crossing the mountains and seven seas to seek and discover myself. People called me wise; rather I should have been called stupid, searching for myself outside instead of being still and looking within, becoming aware of what I already am. Finally I realized that I was the most extravagant vagabond I had ever met for wasting my breath and time searching for myself here, there, and everywhere.

§

At Thy Holy Feet

Child am I of a sage of the mountain.
Free spirit am I; light walks by my side.
Fearless live I above glacial fountain,
In seclusion of Himalayan cavern reside.

With snowy weather beating around me,
Ascending the peaks of the mountains I go.
No one talks with me, no one walks with me,
As I cross streams and tramp glacial snow.

I roam in the mountains that hark to the skies,
And of silence have made me a friend.
My Love whispers to me with silent replies.
And guided by these I ascend.

These days dwell I in a foreign land,
Missing the Ganga* and silvery sand.
Holding within my sacred bosom,
Thy blessing, grace, and ancient wisdom,

Offering my life at thy holy feet,
Loving all—selfless and complete.

§

*The holy River Ganges

About the Author

Born in 1925 in northern India, Swami Rama was raised from early childhood by a great Bengali yogi and saint who lived in the foothills of the Himalayas. In his youth he practiced the various disciplines of yoga science and philosophy in the traditional monasteries of the Himalayas and studied with many spiritual adepts, including Mahatma Gandhi, Sri Aurobindo, and Rabindranath Tagore. He also traveled to Tibet to study with his grandmaster.

He received his higher education at Prayaga, Varanasi, and Oxford University, England. At the age of twenty-four he became Shankaracharya of Karvirpitham in South India, the highest spiritual position in India. During this term he had a tremendous impact on the spiritual customs of that time: he dispensed with useless formalities and rituals, made it possible for all segments of society to worship in the temples, and encouraged the instruction of women in meditation. He renounced the dignity and prestige of this high office in 1952 to return to the Himalayas to intensify his yogic practices.

After completing an intense meditative practice in the cave monasteries, he emerged with the determination to serve humanity, particularly to bring the teachings of the East to the West. With the encouragement of his master, Swami Rama began his task by studying Western philosophy and psychology. He worked as a medical consultant in London and assisted in parapsychological research in Moscow. He then returned to India, where he established an ashram in Rishikesh. He completed his degree in homeopathy at the medical college in Darbhanga in 1960. He came to the United States in 1969, bringing his knowledge and wisdom to the West. His teachings combine Eastern spirituality with modern Western therapies.

Swami Rama was a freethinker, guided by his direct experience and inner wisdom, and he encouraged his students to be guided in the same way. He often told them, "I am a messenger, delivering the wisdom of the Himalayan sages of my tradition. My job is to introduce you to the teacher within."

Swami Rama came to America upon the invitation of Dr. Elmer Green of the Menninger Foundation of Topeka, Kansas, as a consultant in a research project investigating the voluntary control of involuntary states. He participated in experiments that helped to revolutionize scientific thinking about the relationship between body and mind, amazing scientists by his demonstrating, under laboratory conditions, precise conscious control of autonomic physical responses and mental functioning, feats previously thought to be impossible.

Swami Rama founded the Himalayan International Institute of Yoga Science and Philosophy, the Himalayan Institute Hospital Trust in India, and many centers throughout the world. He is the author of numerous books on health, meditation, and the yogic scriptures. Swami Rama left his body in November 1996.

The main building of the Institute headquarters, near Honesdale, Pennsylvania.

The Himalayan Institute

Founded in 1971 by Swami Rama, the Himalayan Institute has been dedicated to helping people grow physically, mentally, and spiritually by combining the best knowledge of both the East and the West.

Our international headquarters is located on a beautiful 400-acre campus in the rolling hills of the Pocono Mountains of northeastern Pennsylvania. The atmosphere here is one to foster growth, increased inner awareness, and calm. Our grounds provide a wonderfully peaceful and healthy setting for our seminars and extended programs. Students from around the world join us here to attend programs in such diverse areas as hatha yoga, meditation, stress reduction, Ayurveda, nutrition, Eastern philosophy, psychology, and other subjects. Whether the programs are for weekend meditation retreats, week-long seminars on spirituality, months-long residential programs, or holistic health services, the attempt here is to provide an environment of gentle inner progress. We invite you to join with us in the ongoing process of personal growth and development.

The Institute is a nonprofit organization. Your membership in the Institute helps to support its programs. Please call or write for information on becoming a member.

Institute Programs, Services, and Facilities

Institute programs share an emphasis on conscious holistic living and personal self-development, including:

- Special weekend or extended seminars to teach skills and techniques for increasing your ability to be healthy and enjoy life
- Meditation retreats and advanced meditation and philosophical instruction
- Vegetarian cooking and nutritional training
- Hatha yoga and exercise workshops
- Residential programs for self-development
- Holistic health services and Ayurvedic Rejuvenation Programs through the Institute's Center for Health and Healing.

A *Quarterly Guide to Programs and Other Offerings* is free within the USA. To request a copy, or for further information, call 800-822-4547 or 570-253-5551, fax 570-253-9078, email bqinfo@himalayaninstitute.org, write the Himalayan Institute, RR 1 Box 400, Honesdale, PA 18431-9706 USA or visit our website at www.himalayaninstitute.org.

The Himalayan Institute Press

The Himalayan Institute Press has long been regarded as "The Resource for Holistic Living." We publish dozens of titles, as well as audio and video tapes, that offer practical methods for living harmoniously and achieving inner balance. Our approach addresses the whole person—body, mind, and spirit—integrating the latest scientific knowledge with ancient healing and self-development techniques.

As such, we offer a wide array of titles on physical and psychological health and well-being, spiritual growth through meditation and other yogic practices, as well as translations of yogic scriptures.

Our sidelines include the Japa Kit for meditation practice, the Neti™ Pot, the ideal tool for sinus and allergy sufferers, and The Breath Pillow,™ a unique tool for learning health-supportive diaphragmatic breathing.

Subscriptions are available to a bimonthly magazine, *Yoga International*, which offers thought-provoking articles on all aspects of meditation and yoga, including yoga's sister science, Ayurveda.

For a free catalog call 800-822-4547 or 570-253-5551, email hibooks@himalayaninstitute.org, fax 570-253-6360, write the Himalayan Institute Press, RR 1 Box 405, Honesdale, PA 18431-9709 USA or visit our website at www.himalayaninstitute.org.